BIBLE STUDIES

Jesus: Understanding His Death and Resurrection

Kay Arthur & David Arthur

PRECEPT MINISTRIES INTERNATIONAL

WATERBROOK
PRESS

Jesus: Understanding His Death and Resurrection

All Scripture quotations are taken from the New American Standard Bible®. Copyright © 1960, 1962, 1963, 1968, 1971, 1972, 1973, 1975, 1977, 1995 by the Lockman Foundation. Used by permission. (www.Lockman.org).

Italics in Scripture quotations reflect the authors' added emphasis.

Trade Paperback ISBN 978-1-60142-804-2
eBook ISBN 978-1-60142-805-9

Copyright © 2015 by Precept Ministries International

Cover design by The Designworks Group

Published in the United States by WaterBrook, an imprint of the Crown Publishing Group, a division of Penguin Random House LLC, New York.

WaterBrook® and its deer colophon are registered trademarks of Penguin Random House LLC.

Printed in the United States of America
2018

10 9 8 7 6 5

Special Sales
Most WaterBrook books are available at special quantity discounts when purchased in bulk by corporations, organizations, and special-interest groups. Custom imprinting or excerpting can also be done to fit special needs. For information, please e-mail specialmarketscms @penguinrandomhouse.com or call 1-800-603-7051.

CONTENTS

This small-group study is for people who are interested in learning for themselves more about what the Bible says on various subjects, but who have only limited time to meet together. It's ideal, for example, for a lunch group at work, an early morning men's group, a young mothers' group meeting in a home, a Sunday-school class, or even family devotions. (It's also ideal for small groups that typically have longer meeting times—such as evening groups or Saturday morning groups—but want to devote only a portion of their time together to actual study, while reserving the rest for prayer, fellowship, or other activities.)

This book is designed so that all the group's participants will complete each lesson's study activities *at the same time*. Discussing your insights drawn from what God says about the subject reveals exciting, life-impacting truths.

Although it's a group study, you'll need a facilitator to lead the study and keep the discussion moving. If *you* are your group's facilitator, the leader, here are some helpful points for making your job easier:

- Go through the lesson and mark the text before you lead the group. This will give you increased familiarity with the material and will enable you to facilitate the group with greater ease. It may be easier for you to lead the group through the instructions for marking if you, as a leader, choose a specific color for each symbol you mark.

- As you lead the group, start at the beginning of the text and simply read it aloud in the order it appears in the lesson, including the Insight boxes that appear throughout. Work through the lesson together, observing and discussing what you learn. As you read the Scripture verses, have the group say aloud the word they are marking in the text.

- The discussion questions are there simply to help you cover the material. As the class moves into the discussion, many times you will find that they will cover the questions on their own. Remember, the discussion questions are there to guide the group through the topic, not to squelch discussion.

- Remember how important it is for people to verbalize their answers and discoveries. This greatly strengthens their personal understanding of each week's lesson. Try to ensure that everyone has plenty of opportunity to contribute to each week's discussions.

- Keep the discussion moving. This may mean spending more time on some parts of the study than on others. If necessary, you should feel free to spread out a lesson over more than one session. However, remember that you don't want to slow the pace too much. It's much better to leave everyone wanting more than to have people dropping out because of declining interest.

- If the validity or accuracy of some of the answers seems questionable, you can gently and cheerfully remind the group to stay focused on the truth of the Scriptures. Your object is to learn what the Bible says, not to engage in human philosophy. Simply stick with the Scriptures and give God the opportunity to speak. His Word *is* truth (John 17:17)!

JESUS: UNDERSTANDING HIS DEATH AND RESURRECTION

A nd the sons of Israel sighed because of the bondage, and they cried out; and their cry for help because of their bondage rose up to God" (Exodus 2:23).

Exodus, the second book of the Bible, tells us that after four hundred years of bondage in Egypt, the sons of Israel groaned to God and He heard them. As their cries arose in His ears, He remembered His covenant with Abraham, Isaac, and Jacob. It was His time to set His people free, to deliver them from slavery. The sign for deliverance would be the blood of a spotless lamb painted on the doorpost of each Israelite house. The angel of death, seeing the blood, would "pass over" the house. Wherever the blood was absent, the firstborn male in the household would die—and Pharoah finally would be convinced to let God's people go!

Are you sighing, groaning because you want to be free from that which enslaves you?

Or maybe you have friends, family, associates who want what you have: freedom from bondage to sin, peace with God. Reconciliation! The power to live a life pleasing to God!

Whether the cries for deliverance are your own or come from someone you know, we have good news! This good news is the gospel, the account of the death and resurrection of the Son of God, who became the Son of Man. Through the next six weeks you will discover and study for yourself the record of this story in a way that will help you know that you know what God has written in His Word.

It's truth—truth that sets the captive free!

As the time of Passover again drew near, Jesus and His disciples gathered in Jerusalem with thousands of other faithful Jews.

However, this Passover was to be unlike any that had ever preceded it or was to come. This Passover would mark a new era, launched by an event that would change the course of history and clear the way for each of us to live in union with God.

As we read through Mark's description of this Passover, please know that what you believe and do with the truths we are about to study will determine your destiny. Your decision to either live by God's precepts or ignore them will set your course for eternity. Your decision to believe or not to believe will bring either life eternal or eternal damnation.

That is a weighty statement, but instead of taking our word for it, let's get into the Word of God to see what He says.

MARK 14:1–11

¹ Now the Passover and Unleavened Bread were two days away; and the chief priests and the scribes were seeking how to seize Him by stealth and kill Him;

² for they were saying, "Not during the festival, otherwise there might be a riot of the people."

³ While He was in Bethany at the home of Simon the leper, and reclining at the table, there came a woman with an alabaster vial of very costly perfume of pure nard; and she broke the vial and poured it over His head.

OBSERVE

Leader: Read Mark 14:1–11 aloud. As you do, have the group mark the text in the following ways:

- *Circle all references to* **time,** *including mentions of annual feasts such as* **Passover** *and* **Unleavened Bread.**
- *Mark every reference to* **Jesus** *with a cross:* †. *In the same way, mark any pronouns such as* **Him, He,** *and* **My** *that refer to Jesus Christ. Since you'll be marking references to Jesus so often over the next six weeks, you may prefer to use a particular color to mark the references to Him so they pop on the page.*
- *Place a big* **W** *over every reference to* **the woman.**
- *Mark every reference to* **money** *with a dollar sign:* **$**

As you read the text, it's helpful to have the group say the key words aloud as they mark them. This way everyone will be sure they are marking every occurrence of the word, including any synonymous words or phrases. Do this throughout the study.

DISCUSS

• According to verses 1 and 2, what plot was being hatched? What was the concern of the conspirators?

• According to verses 3–5, where was Jesus? Summarize what happened.

• Look at where you marked *the woman*. What do you learn about her?

INSIGHT

A *denarii* was a day's wage; therefore, the perfume was valued at almost an entire year's income. The woman's extravagant offering would have been shocking to the witnesses.

• According to Jesus' comment in verse 8, what was going to happen to Him?

4 But some were indignantly remarking to one another, "Why has this perfume been wasted?

5 "For this perfume might have been sold for over three hundred denarii, and the money given to the poor." And they were scolding her.

6 But Jesus said, "Let her alone; why do you bother her? She has done a good deed to Me.

7 "For you always have the poor with you, and whenever you wish you can do good to them; but you do not always have Me.

8 "She has done what she could; she

has anointed My body beforehand for the burial.

9 "Truly I say to you, wherever the gospel is preached in the whole world, what this woman has done will also be spoken of in memory of her."

10 Then Judas Iscariot, who was one of the twelve, went off to the chief priests in order to betray Him to them.

11 They were glad when they heard this, and promised to give him money. And he began seeking how to betray Him at an opportune time.

• According to verses 6–9, what did Jesus think about the woman's extravagant outpouring? What was she doing?

• Why were her actions so commendable?

• What actions are described in verses 10–11? What contrast do you see here with the account of the woman's perfume?

• Describe a time you've witnessed someone's extravagant gift to Jesus—not necessarily a gift of monetary value but something that clearly required a sacrifice. What does such sacrificial giving indicate about our priorities?

OBSERVE

Leader: Read Mark 14:12–21 aloud. Have the group mark the text as follows:

- *Circle all references to* **time**, *such as* **Passover** *and* **day of Unleavened Bread.**
- *Mark each reference to* **Jesus**, *including all pronouns and synonyms such as* **Son of Man.**
- *Put a big* **X** *over every reference to* **betrayal** *and* **the betrayer.**

INSIGHT

Every year Israel was commanded to celebrate the Passover, which commemorated Israel's exodus from Egypt. This liberation of God's covenant people after they had been slaves in Egypt for four hundred years would become the first of three prophetic feasts celebrated annually by Israel: Passover, Pentecost, and Tabernacles.

Exodus 12, the account of the first Passover, gives a prophetic picture of the deliverance that was to

MARK 14:12–21

12 On the first day of Unleavened Bread, when the Passover lamb was being sacrificed, His disciples said to Him, "Where do You want us to go and prepare for You to eat the Passover?"

13 And He sent two of His disciples and said to them, "Go into the city, and a man will meet you carrying a pitcher of water; follow him;

14 and wherever he enters, say to the owner of the house, 'The Teacher says, "Where is My guest room in which I may eat the Passover with My disciples?"'

15 "And he himself will show you a large upper room furnished and ready; prepare for us there."

16 The disciples went out and came to the city, and found it just as He had told them; and they prepared the Passover.

17 When it was evening He came with the twelve.

18 As they were reclining at the table and eating, Jesus said, "Truly I say to you that one of you will betray Me—one who is eating with Me."

19 They began to be grieved and to say to

come through the blood of an unblemished lamb.

Each household of Israelites was to select an unblemished male lamb on the tenth of the first month of the year, observe it to be sure there was no defect in it, and then kill the lamb at twilight on the fourteenth day. The lamb was to be roasted with fire and eaten with unleavened bread and bitter herbs.

The blood of the lamb was to be put on the doorposts and the lintel of the entrance to their house. That night when the angel of death came to kill the firstborn male, if it saw the blood of the lamb, it would pass over the house.

The Feast of Passover comprised three feasts: Passover, Unleavened Bread, and Firstfruits. All three gave the prophetic picture of the death and resurrection of "the Lamb of God who takes away the sin of the world!" (John 1:29, 36).

DISCUSS

• On what day did the events of this passage occur?

• What were Jesus' instructions, and why did He give them? Think about it: what did Jesus know was going to happen that the disciples did not yet realize?

• If Jesus knew this, what does that indicate about the extent of His knowledge?

• How can knowing this about Jesus help shape your perspective day by day?

• What do you learn about the Son of Man in verse 21?

• Describe the reaction of the disciples to Jesus' statement in verse 18. What does this tell you?

• Has Mark ever told us who the betrayer would be? If so, when and where was that revealed?

Him one by one, "Surely not I?"

20 And He said to them, "It is one of the twelve, one who dips with Me in the bowl.

21 "For the Son of Man is to go just as it is written of Him; but woe to that man by whom the Son of Man is betrayed! It would have been good for that man if he had not been born."

• Who was this individual, and why was he betraying Jesus?

MARK 14:22–26

22 While they were eating, He took some bread, and after a blessing He broke it, and gave it to them, and said, "Take it; this is My body."

23 And when He had taken a cup and given thanks, He gave it to them, and they all drank from it.

24 And He said to them, "This is My blood of the covenant, which is poured out for many.

25 "Truly I say to you, I will never again drink of the fruit of

OBSERVE

Leader: Read Mark 14:22–26 aloud. Have the group do the following:

- *Circle all references to **time**, such as **while** and **after**.*
- *Mark each of the pronouns referring to **Jesus**.*
- *Double underline any indication of __geographical location__.*
- *Draw a box around the word **kingdom**, like this: ☐*

DISCUSS

• What happened during the Passover meal? What did Jesus do?

• What did Jesus say about the bread?

• What did He say about the cup?

the vine until that day when I drink it new in the kingdom of God."

• What did Jesus declare in verse 25? Note especially the timing.

26 After singing a hymn, they went out to the Mount of Olives.

INSIGHT

A *covenant* is a solemn, binding agreement. The Old Testament term used for making a covenant is *karat berit,* which means "to cut a covenant." It refers to the ritual sacrifice, the shedding of blood that occurs in making a covenant. Blood was shed in the establishment of the Old Covenant of the Law and in the New Covenant of grace. Under the Old Covenant it was the blood of an animal; under the New, it was the blood of God's Lamb, the Son of Man, the Son of God (Hebrews 10:1–18; 1 Peter 1:18–19).

MATTHEW 26:27–28

27 And when He had taken a cup and given thanks, He gave it to them, saying, "Drink from it, all of you;

28 for this is My blood of the covenant, which is poured out for many for forgiveness of sins."

OBSERVE

Before we bring this week's study to a close, let's look at what Matthew recorded in his gospel about the cup of wine at the Passover feast Jesus shared with His disciples.

Leader: Read Matthew 26:27–28 aloud. Have the group say and mark...

- ***blood*** *with three drops, like this:* **˙•˙**
- ***covenant*** *with a box:* ☐
- ***sins*** *with a big* **S.**

DISCUSS

- What did the content of the cup represent, and why was it being poured out?

- What did Jesus ask His disciples to do?

- What would drinking the cup of this covenant indicate?

WRAP IT UP

About six hundred years before Jesus celebrated His final Passover meal with the disciples, God made a promise to His people, through the prophet Jeremiah, that a time was coming when He would deal with their sin once and for all. It was the promise of the new covenant.

> "Behold, days are coming," declares the LORD, "when I will make a new covenant with the house of Israel and with the house of Judah.… I will put My law within them and on their heart I will write it; and I will be their God, and they shall be My people. They will not teach again, each man his neighbor and each man his brother, saying, 'Know the LORD,' for they will all know Me, from the least of them to the greatest of them," declares the LORD, "for I will forgive their iniquity, and their sin I will remember no more." (Jeremiah 31:31, 33–34)

God promised to give His people a new covenant. Not like the covenant of the Law He made with them after He brought them out of Egypt—a covenant they broke over and over again. Instead, this new covenant would write God's Law on their hearts. No longer would they have to say to one another, "Know the LORD." They would all know Him, from the least of them to the greatest, for He would forgive their iniquity and remember their sin no more.

Now, as Jesus broke bread with His disciples, that long-ago prophecy was about to be fulfilled. The blood of a sacrificial Lamb was to be poured out. The cutting of a new covenant would bring salvation and forgiveness for all those who believed on Him.

Beloved, do you realize that only Jesus—the Son of God, the Son of Man—can offer forgiveness of all our sin through the shedding of His blood? Do you see and believe this beautiful truth?

By repenting of your sins and believing in Jesus alone you will be forgiven and receive the gift of the Holy Spirit! This is the true message of what the world celebrates as Easter. It is more than painting and hiding Easter eggs, eating chocolate bunnies, buying new outfits, and going to church. Easter is the celebration of Jesus' resurrection. The resurrection was proof that the shedding of Jesus' blood for the payment of our sins was accepted by our just and righteous God. Death could not hold Him. Jesus rose on the third day. And those who believe in Him are given the gift of eternal life. Death cannot hold us! Because Jesus, the Son of Man, lives, we will live also—with Him. Forever!

Do you believe? Have you repented of your sins and sought God's forgiveness through His Son? Have you passed from death to life?

One of our favorite places to go in Jerusalem is the Garden of Gethsemane on the Mount of Olives. *Gethsemane* means "oil press." In that garden today, under the protection of a tall iron fence, you'll find large gnarled olive trees that are believed to date back to the time of Jesus. It's truly amazing to think they still exist, but that's the nature of olive trees.

Years ago there was no fence. We could roam the little garden with its wild red poppies in late spring. Then standing under the shade of those ancient trees, we would read aloud God's account of what happened after Jesus and the eleven left the large upper room and made their way across the Kidron valley to the garden (John 18:1).

Let's see what Mark tells us in his gospel about the events of this infamous night in history.

OBSERVE

Jesus, having celebrated His final Passover, knew that His hour had come.

Leader: Read Mark 14:26–31 aloud. Have the group do the following:

- *Circle all references to* (time) *or* **the chronological order of events,** *such as* **after.**
- *Double underline any references to* **geographical location.**
- *Mark all references to* **Jesus,** *including pronouns and synonyms such as* **shepherd.**

MARK 14:26–31

26 After singing a hymn, they went out to the Mount of Olives.

27 And Jesus said to them, "You will all fall away, because it is written, 'I will strike down the shepherd, and the sheep shall be scattered.'

28 "But after I have been raised, I will go ahead of you to Galilee."

29 But Peter said to Him, "Even though all may fall away, yet I will not."

30 And Jesus said to him, "Truly I say to you, that this very night, before a rooster crows twice, you your-

• *Mark the references to* **the disciples** *with an arrow:* ⟶ *Watch carefully for synonyms and pronouns such as* **they, them, you.**

DISCUSS

• According to verse 26, where did Jesus and His disciples go? Look at the map below so you have an idea of the geographical setting.

Jerusalem of the New Testament

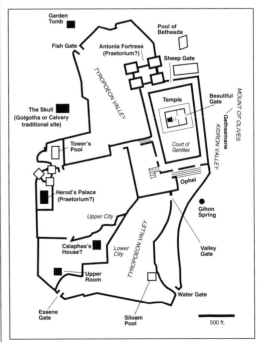

• What did Jesus say in verses 27–28 was about to happen to Him? To the disciples?

• How did Peter respond to Jesus' declaration?

• What did Jesus say specifically to Peter in verse 30, and how did Peter respond?

• What does verse 31 tell you about the other apostles?

• When you stop and think about what you've just read, what does it tell you about Jesus?

self will deny Me three times."

31 But Peter kept saying insistently, "Even if I have to die with You, I will not deny You!" And they all were saying the same thing also.

ZECHARIAH 13:7

"Awake, O sword, against My Shepherd, and against the man, My Associate," declares the LORD of hosts. "Strike the Shepherd that the sheep may be scattered."

OBSERVE

Let's take a moment to read the prophecy Jesus referred to in Mark 14:27. It is found in Zechariah 13:7, written more than five hundred years before the events recorded in Mark 14. God watches over His Word to perform it!

Leader: Read Zechariah 13:7 aloud and have the group...

- *put a cross over every reference to **the Shepherd, the man, Associate:** †*
- *mark **sheep** with an arrow as you did* the disciples, *since sheep follow their shepherd:* ⟶

DISCUSS

- What did you learn from marking each reference to the Shepherd?

• The Bible is the best interpreter of itself. So comparing scripture with scripture and considering the context of Jesus' quote of Zechariah 13:7, what is meant by the phrase "strike the Shepherd"?

• What would then happen to the sheep?

• And who are these sheep?

• Who called for these events to happen?

• Now, having looked at Zechariah 13:7, what was Jesus showing the disciples when He quoted this passage?

MARK 14:32-42

32 They came to a place named Gethsemane; and He said to His disciples, "Sit here until I have prayed."

33 And He took with Him Peter and James and John, and began to be very distressed and troubled.

34 And He said to them, "My soul is deeply grieved to the point of death; remain here and keep watch."

35 And He went a little beyond them, and fell to the ground and began to pray that if it were possible, the hour might pass Him by.

36 And He was saying, "Abba! Father! All things are possible for

OBSERVE

Leader: *Read Mark 14:32–42. Once again, have the group…*

- *circle all indications of **time**.*
- *double underline any references to **geographical location.***
- *mark all references to **Jesus.***
- *mark all references to **prayer** like this:* prayer

Leader: *Read Mark 14:32–42 again, and this time have the group…*

- *put a check mark over every reference to **watch(ing)**: ✓*
- *mark the word **betrayed** with a big **X.***

DISCUSS

- Where was Jesus in this passage? Who was with Him?

- What did Jesus do in Gethsemane? What did He ask God?

- How many times in this passage are we told that Jesus prayed?

- What insight, if any, does this give you into what Jesus was experiencing?

- What did Jesus ask Peter, James, and John to do, and why?

- What do you learn about the spirit and the flesh in verse 38?

You; remove this cup from Me; yet not what I will, but what You will."

37 And He came and found them sleeping, and said to Peter, "Simon, are you asleep? Could you not keep watch for one hour?

38 "Keep watching and praying that you may not come into temptation; the spirit is willing, but the flesh is weak."

39 Again He went away and prayed, saying the same words.

40 And again He came and found them sleeping, for their eyes were very heavy; and they did not know what to answer Him.

41 And He came the third time, and said to them, "Are you still sleeping and resting? It is enough; the hour has come; behold, the Son of Man is being betrayed into the hands of sinners.

42 "Get up, let us be going; behold, the one who betrays Me is at hand!"

LUKE 22:41–46

41 And He withdrew from them about a stone's throw, and He knelt down and began to pray,

42 saying, "Father, if You are willing, remove this cup from Me; yet not My will, but Yours be done."

• How are you to deal with the flesh, based on what you read here, and how would this help you when you are tempted?

OBSERVE

How great was the distress of Jesus as He prayed to the Father that evening? Matthew tells us in his gospel that Jesus asked God three times to "remove this cup." Let's compare what is said in Mark with what Luke the physician wrote in his gospel account.

Leader: Read Luke 22:41–46 and mark...
- *every pronoun that refers to **Jesus.***
- *references to **prayer** like this:* (prayer)

DISCUSS

• What do you learn about Jesus in these verses?

• Luke tells us that Jesus sweat so profusely that, as He prayed, His sweat became like drops of blood, falling to the ground, and that an angel was sent to strengthen Him. What insight does this give you into Jesus' emotional and physical state at this time?

INSIGHT

Hematidrosis is a Greek word composed of two roots, both found in Luke 22:44: "His sweat [*idros*] became like drops of blood [*aima*]." Hematidrosis is the process or action (*-sis*) of sweating blood. This rare condition of sweating blood through the pores of various places in the body can be triggered by intense stress like the immediate threat of death.

---

43 Now an angel from heaven appeared to Him, strengthening Him.

44 And being in agony He was praying very fervently; and His sweat became like drops of blood, falling down upon the ground.

45 When He rose from prayer, He came to the disciples and found them sleeping from sorrow,

46 and said to them, "Why are you sleeping? Get up and pray that you may not enter into temptation."

• Judging by the physical response of Jesus' body and the words of His prayer, how intense was this moment and this decision for Him?

• Where would Jesus' decision ultimately lead Him?

WRAP IT UP

The Shepherd is about to be struck. Ultimately, the hand behind the strike is the hand of His Father so that He, God, can become your Father.

Hundreds of years earlier, Isaiah 53:10 prophetically pointed ahead to this very scene: "But the LORD was *pleased* to crush Him, putting Him to grief." Perhaps one of the most challenging aspects to Jesus' sacrifice is the role of the Father in it all. It can be hard for us to comprehend the idea that God the Father had such an active part in putting His own Son to death. But there was no other way for our sin to be atoned for.

This is why Jesus said, *"Not My will, but Yours be done"* (Luke 22:42). There was no other way. So "He humbled Himself by becoming obedient to the point of death, even death on a cross" (Philippians 2:8).

And with that, the Father and the Son leave us an example of obedience and of love.

If Jesus loved us so much that He was willing to obey His Father even unto death, how far will we go in obeying our Lord and Savior, Jesus Christ?

If the Father was pleased to crush His Son in Gethsemane—for our salvation—just how amazing is His love for you and me?

Sometimes when we read the Bible, we read the words, but we don't stop and think about what God has said—and why He tells us what He does. Every word in the Bible is His, and every word has a purpose.

At this point in the gospel of Mark, God wants you to know what His Son, who knew no sin, endured for you. The writer of the book of Hebrews tells us Jesus despised the shame (12:2). But He took it for you because it was the only way He could become your Savior, One who understands your shame and your pain.

Let's see for ourselves what happened after Jesus went to rouse His disciples for a third time.

OBSERVE

As we read the next portion of Mark 14, let's put ourselves in context by starting at verse 41.

Leader: Read Mark 14:41–52 aloud. Have the group do the following:
- *Circle references to **time**, such as **after**.*
- *Double underline anything that indicates **location.***
- *Mark all references to **Jesus.***
- *Mark with a big **X** all references to **betrayal**, including the betrayer, **Judas.***

MARK 14:41–52

41 And He came the third time, and said to them, "Are you still sleeping and resting? It is enough; the hour has come; behold, the Son of Man is being betrayed into the hands of sinners.

42 "Get up, let us be going; behold, the one who betrays Me is at hand!"

43 Immediately while He was still speaking, Judas, one of the twelve, came up accompanied by a crowd with swords and clubs, who were from the chief priests and the scribes and the elders.

44 Now he who was betraying Him had given them a signal, saying, "Whomever I kiss, He is the one; seize Him and lead Him away under guard."

45 After coming, Judas immediately went to Him, saying, "Rabbi!" and kissed Him.

46 They laid hands on Him and seized Him.

47 But one of those who stood by drew his sword, and struck the

DISCUSS

• How did Jesus identify Himself in verse 41?

• How did He characterize what was about to happen?

• What did you learn from marking references to betrayal?

• Why is betrayal so painful? Have you ever been betrayed? What was that like? How did you feel, and how did you deal with it?

• Read verse 50 aloud. Who does the "all" include, and what does that tell you about Jesus' situation?

slave of the high priest and cut off his ear.

48 And Jesus said to them, "Have you come out with swords and clubs to arrest Me, as you would against a robber?

49 "Every day I was with you in the temple teaching, and you did not seize Me; but this has taken place to fulfill the Scriptures."

50 And they all left Him and fled.

51 A young man was following Him, wearing nothing but a linen sheet over his naked body; and they seized him.

52 But he pulled free of the linen sheet and escaped naked.

MARK 14:53-65

53 They led Jesus away to the high priest; and all the chief priests and the elders and the scribes gathered together.

54 Peter had followed Him at a distance, right into the courtyard of the high priest; and he was sitting with the officers and warming himself at the fire.

55 Now the chief priests and the whole Council kept trying to obtain testimony against Jesus to put Him to death, and they were not finding any.

56 For many were giving false testimony against Him, but their

OBSERVE

While Mark did not specify where Jesus was taken after the Garden of Gethsemane, we know from the gospels of Matthew and Luke that they led Him to the house of Caiaphas, the high priest.

Leader: Read Mark 14:53–65 aloud. Have the group...
- *mark every reference to **Jesus**.*
- *mark every reference to **testimony** or **testifying** with a capital* **T.**

DISCUSS

- Let's put ourselves in the broad context of these verses: Where was Jesus, why was He there, and what was happening? Describe how He was treated.

- Who was gathered together against Him?

- Locate the house of Caiaphas on the map of Jerusalem near the bottom left, close to the Upper Room.

Jerusalem of the New Testament

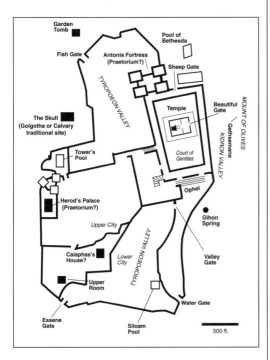

• Look at each place you marked references to testimony. What were the specific testimonies given by those accusing Jesus? Were they valid? Explain your answer.

• What did the high priest do in verse 60? What do you think he expected Jesus to do?

testimony was not consistent.

57 Some stood up and began to give false testimony against Him, saying,

58 "We heard Him say, 'I will destroy this temple made with hands, and in three days I will build another made without hands.'"

59 Not even in this respect was their testimony consistent.

60 The high priest stood up and came forward and questioned Jesus, saying, "Do You not answer? What is it that these men are testifying against You?"

61 But He kept silent and did not answer. Again the high priest was questioning Him, and saying to Him, "Are You the Christ, the Son of the Blessed One?"

62 And Jesus said, "I am; and you shall see the Son of Man sitting at the right hand of Power, and coming with the clouds of heaven."

63 Tearing his clothes, the high priest said, "What further need do we have of witnesses?

64 "You have heard the blasphemy; how does it seem to you?" And they all condemned Him to be deserving of death.

INSIGHT

The Council mentioned in Mark 14:55 is the *Sanhedrin*—from the Greek roots *sun* (together) and *era* (seat).

Comprising seventy members from the Pharisees and Sadducees plus a high priest (Caiaphas in Jesus' day), this body was the highest Jewish court for settling religious legal matters. However, it could be overruled by the Romans. John recorded an example of their limited authority when the Jews told Pilate, "We are not permitted to put anyone to death" (John 18:31).

• According to verse 61, how did Jesus respond to the high priest's actions? What did His answer reveal?

• What did the high priest ask Jesus in verse 61, and how did Jesus respond?

• When Jesus answered by quoting Scripture, how did the high priest react? What did he accuse Jesus of?

• The Jews were waiting for Messiah (the Christ) to come in His kingdom, so what was Jesus telling them?

• What was done to Jesus in the house of Caiaphas with the knowledge and permission of the Council?

OBSERVE

Several passages in the Old Testament seem to give us prophetic insight into the suffering of the Messiah, Christ. Let's look, for example, at a few verses in Isaiah 50.

Leader: *Read Isaiah 50:5–7 aloud.*
   • *Have the group mark the pronouns I, My, Me as they've marked Jesus.*

65 Some began to spit at Him, and to blindfold Him, and to beat Him with their fists, and to say to Him, "Prophesy!" And the officers received Him with slaps in the face.

ISAIAH 50:5–7

5 The Lord GOD has opened My ear; and I was not disobedient nor did I turn back.

6 I gave My back to those who strike Me, and My cheeks to those who pluck out the beard; I did

not cover My face
from humiliation and
spitting.

⁷ For the Lord GOD
helps Me, therefore,
I am not disgraced;
therefore, I have set
My face like flint, and
I know that I will not
be ashamed.

DISCUSS

• What do you learn from marking the pronouns?

• What similarities do you see between these verses in Isaiah and what happened to Jesus in the house of Caiaphas?

• If this is a prophecy regarding Christ, what do you learn about His beard from Isaiah? Think about the pain and disgrace of that.

• What does verse 7 tell you about the relationship between the One speaking and God?

• How might knowing this help you walk in obedience to the Lord even in demeaning situations?

OBSERVE

In Mark 14:54, we read that Peter followed Jesus at a distance and ended up in the courtyard of the high priest. There he sat down with the officers who were warming themselves at a fire. Mark now tells us what happened next.

Leader: Read Mark 14:66–72 aloud. Have the group do the following:
- *Circle references to **time**.*
- *Double underline anything that indicates **where**.*
- *Put a big **P** over each reference to **Peter**.*

DISCUSS

- Where was Peter?

- How did Peter respond to being associated with Jesus?

MARK 14:66–72

66 As Peter was below in the courtyard, one of the servant-girls of the high priest came,

67 and seeing Peter warming himself, she looked at him and said, "You also were with Jesus the Nazarene."

68 But he denied it, saying, "I neither know nor understand what you are talking about." And he went out onto the porch.

69 The servant-girl saw him, and began once more to say to the bystanders, "This is one of them!"

70 But again he denied it. And after a little while the

bystanders were again saying to Peter, "Surely you are one of them, for you are a Galilean too."

71 But he began to curse and swear, "I do not know this man you are talking about!"

72 Immediately a rooster crowed a second time. And Peter remembered how Jesus had made the remark to him, "Before a rooster crows twice, you will deny Me three times." And he began to weep.

• What does verse 72 tell you about Jesus?

• If Jesus knew that about Peter, what does He know about us and what lies in our future?

• How does that make you feel?

OBSERVE

Let's look at two cross-references and see what lessons we might find to help us in our relationship with the Lord.

Leader: Read Luke 22:28–34 aloud. Have the group…

- *mark every reference to Jesus, including synonyms and pronouns.*
- *draw an arrow under every you that refers to the disciples collectively:*

$\longrightarrow$

- *put a big P over each specific reference to Simon Peter, watching carefully for the pronoun you.*

DISCUSS

- Look at each place you marked a *you* in reference to the disciples. What do you learn about them, and what were they promised?

LUKE 22:28–34

28 "You are those who have stood by Me in My trials;

29 and just as My Father has granted Me a kingdom, I grant you

30 that you may eat and drink at My table in My kingdom, and you will sit on thrones judging the twelve tribes of Israel.

31 "Simon, Simon, behold, Satan has demanded permission to sift you like wheat;

32 but I have prayed for you, that your faith may not fail; and you, when once you have turned again, strengthen your brothers."

33 But he said to Him, "Lord, with You I am ready to go both to prison and to death!"

34 And He said, "I say to you, Peter, the rooster will not crow today until you have denied three times that you know Me."

• What did Jesus say about Simon Peter? Don't miss a thing!

• How could Jesus' words to Peter bring the disciple comfort after he later denies knowing Jesus? Is there hope for Peter? Explain your answer.

• How could knowing this give you hope?

• What does this tell you about one of the purposes of prayer?

OBSERVE

Let's see what additional details Luke reveals about Peter's denial of Jesus.

Leader: Read Luke 22:59–62 aloud. Have the group mark…

- *each reference to* **Peter** *with a* **P** *beginning with* **this man** *in verse 59.*
- *every mention of* ***Jesus.***

DISCUSS

- What does Luke tell you that Mark's account did not?

- How did Peter respond in verse 62?

- What is the most significant truth you learned in this lesson? What insight can you apply to your life today?

LUKE 22:59–62

59 After about an hour had passed, another man began to insist, saying, "Certainly this man also was with Him, for he is a Galilean too."

60 But Peter said, "Man, I do not know what you are talking about." Immediately, while he was still speaking, a rooster crowed.

61 The Lord turned and looked at Peter. And Peter remembered the word of the Lord, how He had told him, "Before a rooster crows today, you will deny Me three times."

62 And he went out and wept bitterly.

WRAP IT UP

False accusations and betrayal were a part of Jesus' suffering. Jesus had been accused before, but this time the accusations were being presented in a formal council. Court was being held (although illegally), and Jesus was the accused.

Jesus' words were being used out of context to mean something entirely different from what He said originally. Arguments against Him were inconsistent and full of flaws. When asked directly if He was the Christ, Jesus' next two words sent the Council into a rage, "I am."

Isn't it interesting that the declaration of truth is what angered the people? The long-awaited Messiah had finally arrived, and they wanted to kill Him. The One who is the way, the truth, and the life was being called a liar and blasphemer (John 14:6).

In the moment of trial, Jesus was all alone after His disciples abandoned Him. Peter—who had recently witnessed the Father declare Jesus as His beloved Son on the Mount of Transfiguration—denied knowing Jesus three times. A rooster crow and a look from his Master reminded him he had denied the Son of Man.

Why would Jesus, who knew beforehand what was going to happen with the betrayal of a close friend, submit to such persecution? Why would the One who holds all things together, sustaining every molecule in creation, let Himself be beaten and humiliated? Why? Because Jesus, the Son of God, the Son of Man, came to save sinners, to die for those who were enemies of God, and those who were living without hope. He came to show the Father's love for you and me. Oh, how He showed it!

WEEK FOUR

Jesus had already sweat great drops of blood, walked from the Mount of Olives through the Kidron valley, up the slope of the walled city, and climbed the stone steps to the house of Caiaphas, where He spent a long, painful night. In one evening, Jesus had been illegally tried, falsely accused, blindfolded, mocked, beaten, had His beard pulled out, and then was confined in a cold stone pit for the night.

We step into the story early the next morning, where we learn that, feast or not, the high priest was ready for Jesus to be dead and out of the way—this Jesus who brought nothing but trouble to Israel.

The Council had deemed Jesus worthy of death. However, their power was limited. Rome had the final call, so they must seek the consent of Pilate, the Governor.

OBSERVE

Leader: Read Mark 15:1–5 aloud. Have the group do the following:
- *Circle references to **time.***
- *Mark each reference to **Jesus.***
- *Double underline anything that tells you **where something occurred.***
- *Draw a box around each reference to **Pilate.***

MARK 15:1–5

1 Early in the morning the chief priests with the elders and scribes and the whole Council, immediately held a consultation; and binding Jesus, they led Him away and delivered Him to Pilate.

2 Pilate questioned Him, "Are You the King of the Jews?" And He answered him, "It is as you say."

3 The chief priests began to accuse Him harshly.

4 Then Pilate questioned Him again, saying, "Do You not answer? See how many charges they bring against You!"

INSIGHT

About AD 26, Pontius Pilate became the fifth Roman governor of Judea, holding his position from about AD 26–36. An inscription bearing his name was found at Caesarea on the Mediterranean coast. First-century historians sum up his rule as a set of explosive provocations of the Jews. He was cruel and totally insensitive to all things related to the Jewish culture and religion.

According to biblical scholar James A. Brooks, "By the time Mark wrote his gospel, Pilate was so well-known in Christian circles that he did not need to be described. Although the governors usually resided at Caesarea, they often came to Jerusalem *during the Jewish feast* in order to be at the site should disorder arise among the thousands who came to the feasts."[*]

[*] James A. Brooks, *New American Commentary,* vol. 23, *Mark* (Nashville: Broadman & Holman, 1991), 248–49.

DISCUSS

• According to verse 1, where was Jesus taken?

• What did Pilate ask Jesus, and how did He respond?

• What did the chief priests do?

• How did Jesus, at this point, handle the situation?

5 But Jesus made no further answer; so Pilate was amazed.

LUKE 23:4–16

4 Then Pilate said to the chief priests and the crowds, "I find no guilt in this man."

5 But they kept on insisting, saying, "He stirs up the people, teaching all over Judea, starting from Galilee even as far as this place."

6 When Pilate heard it, he asked whether the man was a Galilean.

7 And when he learned that He belonged to Herod's jurisdiction, he sent Him to Herod, who himself also was in Jerusalem at that time.

8 Now Herod was very glad when he saw

OBSERVE

Luke reveals something else that happened at this time and that gives us further insight about one of the key participants in all of this.

Leader: Read Luke 23:4–16 aloud. Once again, have the group do the following:

- *Circle references to **time.***
- *Mark each reference to **Jesus,** including pronouns and synonyms such as **this man.***
- *Double underline anything that tells you **where something occurred.***
- *Draw a box around each reference to **Pilate.***
- *Underline the references to **Herod.***

INSIGHT

Herod Antipas, the son of Herod the Great, was tetrarch of Galilee (Luke 3:1). He first ruled out of Sepphoris, but later built the city of Tiberias on the Sea of Galilee to make it his new capital.

When he married his brother Phillip's wife, Herodias, John the Baptist accused him publicly and was imprisoned (Mark 6:17). Although he wanted to put John to death, Herod feared the Jews because they believed John was a prophet (Matthew 14:5). But Herodias trapped Herod with his own words and forced him to behead John.

DISCUSS

• Look at the following map of Jerusalem so you can see where Jesus was taken. Pilate was in the area of the Antonia Fortress, believed by many scholars to be the site of the Praetorium.

Jesus; for he had wanted to see Him for a long time, because he had been hearing about Him and was hoping to see some sign performed by Him.

⁹ And he questioned Him at some length; but He answered him nothing.

¹⁰ And the chief priests and the scribes were standing there, accusing Him vehemently.

¹¹ And Herod with his soldiers, after treating Him with contempt and mocking Him, dressed Him in a gorgeous robe and sent Him back to Pilate.

12 Now Herod and Pilate became friends with one another that very day; for before they had been enemies with each other.

13 Pilate summoned the chief priests and the rulers and the people,

14 and said to them, "You brought this man to me as one who incites the people to rebellion, and behold, having examined Him before you, I have found no guilt in this man regarding the charges which you make against Him.

15 "No, nor has Herod, for he sent Him back to us; and behold, nothing

Jerusalem of the New Testament

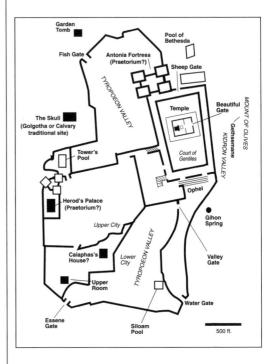

• Who are the main characters in these verses?

• What did Pilate ask about Jesus? What did he do with the information given?

• What do you learn about Herod from this passage, and what did he want to see Jesus do?

• What do you learn about the relationship between Herod and Pilate? What change takes place, and why?

• What brought these two together? If you can, describe a time when you've seen others drawn together in a similar way.

• Have you ever found yourself in such a relationship? If so, how might knowing this help you?

• What actions did others make toward Jesus in this passage? How did He respond? What actions did He take? What does this tell you about Him?

deserving death has been done by Him.

16 "Therefore I will punish Him and release Him."

MARK 15:6–19

6 Now at the feast he used to release for them any one prisoner whom they requested.

7 The man named Barabbas had been imprisoned with the insurrectionists who had committed murder in the insurrection.

8 The crowd went up and began asking him to do as he had been accustomed to do for them.

9 Pilate answered them, saying, "Do you want me to release for you the King of the Jews?"

10 For he was aware that the chief priests had handed Him over because of envy.

OBSERVE

Now that we've witnessed Jesus being sent to Herod, let's return to the gospel of Mark and see what happened when Jesus returned to Pilate.

Leader: Read Mark 15:6–19 aloud. Have the group…
- *put a box around all the references to **Pilate**, beginning with **he** in verse 6.*
- *put a big **C** over each reference to **the crowd**, beginning with **they** in verse 6.*
- *mark each reference to **Jesus**.*

DISCUSS

- What do you learn from marking the references to the crowd? Who was behind their demands?

- What does this tell you about the individuals who made up the crowd?

• Look at the places you marked references to Pilate, and discuss what you see happening to this man in respect to the chief priests and the crowd. What insights, if any, does this give you about Pilate?

• Have you ever felt pressured to please a crowd or individuals with authority or influence? Describe what happened.

INSIGHT

According to Mark 15:16, the soldiers took Jesus to the palace, or the Praetorium. The Praetorium was used as the temporary Roman military headquarters or as the palace in Jerusalem to house the Roman governor. It was either a building next to Herod's palace or next to the Antonia Fortress beside the temple mount complex. See the map on page 46.

11 But the chief priests stirred up the crowd to ask him to release Barabbas for them instead.

12 Answering again, Pilate said to them, "Then what shall I do with Him whom you call the King of the Jews?"

13 They shouted back, "Crucify Him!"

14 But Pilate said to them, "Why, what evil has He done?" But they shouted all the more, "Crucify Him!"

15 Wishing to satisfy the crowd, Pilate released Barabbas for them, and after having Jesus scourged, he handed Him over to be crucified.

16 The soldiers took Him away into the palace (that is, the Praetorium), and they called together the whole Roman cohort.

17 They dressed Him up in purple, and after twisting a crown of thorns, they put it on Him;

18 and they began to acclaim Him, "Hail, King of the Jews!"

19 They kept beating His head with a reed, and spitting on Him, and kneeling and bowing before Him.

• Describe in detail what happened to Jesus in verses 15–19.

• What was Jesus' condition when they "dressed Him up in purple" (verse 17)? What would the robe do to His bloody body, and what would happen to Jesus when they took it off?

INSIGHT

Scourged is translated from the Greek word *phragelloo,* from which we get our English terms *flagellate* and *flagellum.*

The flog, or scourge, was a short whip with leather thongs that terminated with lead or iron balls and sheep bones.

Normally the victim was tied to an upright post, stripped, then whipped on the back, buttocks, and legs. The balls and bones in the whip produced contusions and lacerations (cuts) deep enough to expose skeletal muscle and bone, and eventually led to spurting arterial blood. Often the victim's flesh hung in ribbons, exposing a mass of oozing, bloody tissue. The torturous straps sometimes would disembowel the abdomen.

Between the excruciating pain and blood loss, victims might pass out, go into shock, and often died before they could be crucified.

Scourging is one of the three judgments Isaiah prophesied the Messiah would receive to save us: *pierced* for our transgressions, *crushed* for our iniquities, *scourged* for our healing (Isaiah 53:5).

• Why did they place a crown on Him? What does the text say the crown was made of? What would that do to Jesus' already abused face?

• Now stop and think: Who is this they were mocking and abusing? And why were they doing it?

JOHN 19:1–17

1 Pilate then took Jesus and scourged Him.

2 And the soldiers twisted together a crown of thorns and put it on His head, and put a purple robe on Him;

3 and they began to come up to Him and say, "Hail, King of the Jews!" and to give Him slaps in the face.

4 Pilate came out again and said to them, "Behold, I am bringing Him out to you so that you may know that I find no guilt in Him."

5 Jesus then came out, wearing the crown of thorns and the purple robe. Pilate said to

OBSERVE

Let's go now to the gospel of John for further insight into these events.

Leader: Read John 19:1–17 aloud. Have the group do the following:
- *Circle anything that indicates **when** something happened.*
- *Double underline anything that tells you **where** something occurred.*
- *Mark each reference to **Jesus** and observe carefully where Jesus goes in relationship to Pilate.*
- *Put a box around all the references to **Pilate**.*

DISCUSS

- What happened to Jesus in verses 1–5?

- What did the chief priests want Pilate to do, and why?

• According to verses 7–10, what information compelled Pilate to speak again with Jesus?

• What do you learn in verses 10–11?

• In verse 12, what made Pilate want to release Jesus? What argument did the crowd make against his doing so?

• Do you learn anything from Jesus' answer to Pilate that you can apply to your understanding of God or to the circumstances of life?

them, "Behold, the Man!"

6 So when the chief priests and the officers saw Him, they cried out saying, "Crucify, crucify!" Pilate said to them, "Take Him yourselves and crucify Him, for I find no guilt in Him."

7 The Jews answered him, "We have a law, and by that law He ought to die because He made Himself out to be the Son of God."

8 Therefore when Pilate heard this statement, he was even more afraid;

9 and he entered into the Praetorium again and said to Jesus, "Where are You

from?" But Jesus gave him no answer.

10 So Pilate said to Him, "You do not speak to me? Do You not know that I have authority to release You, and I have authority to crucify You?"

11 Jesus answered, "You would have no authority over Me, unless it had been given you from above; for this reason he who delivered Me to you has the greater sin."

12 As a result of this Pilate made efforts to release Him, but the Jews cried out saying, "If you release this Man, you are no friend of Caesar;

• What was Pilate's dilemma, and what path did he choose?

• God is sovereign. He rules over all, as Jesus said to Pilate. Yet would Pilate be held accountable? How would the mention of "greater sin" in verse 11 help you answer this question?

• Who called for Jesus' death, and why?

• What identification did Pilate make between Jesus and the people?

• Was this title accurate in any way? Did the people agree? Explain your answers.

everyone who makes himself out to be a king opposes Caesar."

13 Therefore when Pilate heard these words, he brought Jesus out, and sat down on the judgment seat at a place called The Pavement, but in Hebrew, Gabbatha.

14 Now it was the day of preparation for the Passover; it was about the sixth hour. And he said to the Jews, "Behold, your King!"

15 So they cried out, "Away with Him, away with Him, crucify Him!" Pilate said to them, "Shall I crucify your King?" The chief priests answered, "We have no king but Caesar."

16 So he then handed Him over to them to be crucified.

17 They took Jesus, therefore, and He went out, bearing His own cross, to the place called the Place of a Skull, which is called in Hebrew, Golgotha.

• So what did Pilate fear more: God, his conscience, or the pressure from the crowd?

• And you? What's your dilemma, and how will you handle it in the framework of your culture?

OBSERVE

Let's close our study by returning to Mark's gospel.

Leader: Read Mark 15:20–22 aloud. Have the group…

- *circle anything that indicates **when** these events happened.*
- *double underline anything that tells you **where** they occurred.*
- *mark each pronoun referring to **Jesus**.*

DISCUSS

- What does Mark tell you that John doesn't?

20 After they had mocked Him, they took the purple robe off Him and put His own garments on Him. And they led Him out to crucify Him.

21 They pressed into service a passer-by coming from the country, Simon of Cyrene (the father of Alexander and Rufus), to bear His cross.

22 Then they brought Him to the place Golgotha, which is translated, Place of a Skull.

WRAP IT UP

Jesus was sent by the Father in the fullness of time, born of a woman, born under the Law. He was tempted, tested in every way that we have been tested—yet without sin (Hebrews 4:15).

Jesus lived as God created mankind to live. He always and only did what pleased His Father. He spoke the Father's words. He did the Father's works. He could legitimately say, "He who has seen Me has seen the Father" (John 14:9). The Son of Man was the Son of God—God in flesh.

Now, remembering that, beloved, think about the holy irony of what was done to the Son of God at the Feast of Passover, the Feast of Unleavened Bread. Consider what happened…

…to our great High Priest: unjustly accused, physically abused, illegally tried by the chief priests who served in His Father's house and made it a den of thieves.

…to the Teacher from Galilee who healed the sick, brought sight to the blind and set the captive free: wounded, blindfolded, and bound by men who sought His demise.

…to the King of kings: forced to wear the robe of an earthly king, demeaned, scorned, and mocked as The King of the Jews.

…to the Son given to us by God who came to take
the government of our lives on His shoulders:
questioned by Pilate, the governor of Judea who
gave in to the cries of the crowd.

…to the Lamb of God who came to bring forgiveness of sins: rejected to make way for the
release of Barabbas, an insurrectionist who had
committed murder.

After these vicious cruelties, death would follow. Beaten and
bloody, Jesus would be taken to the Place of the Skull, where He would
be nailed to a cross—crucified.

As you consider all this, remember that all these events took place
under heaven's authority. Jesus came not to be served but to serve and
to give His life as a ransom for many (Mark 10:45). Jesus said, "Thy
will be done."

May we suggest that, before you meet next week, you find time to
get alone with God. Shut out everything else, turn off your cell phone,
close the door to every distraction—and meditate on what the Father
told you in His Word today. Taking time to think it all over will give
you a greater appreciation for seeing with your own eyes God's account
of the death of His Son—One who was every bit the Son of Man, flesh
and blood with feelings just like ours (Hebrews 4:14–16).

We hear and see so much about death that it can make us insensitive, maybe a little cold, to the death of Jesus Christ. "So He died. Don't we all?"

Yes, we all die, but the death of Jesus Christ was different.

Do you realize that He died for you? And the way He died tells you much about God and about His love for you—as you are about to see.

OBSERVE

Leader: Read Mark 15:22–32 aloud. Have the group do the following:

- *Circle anything that indicates **time.***
- *Double underline anything that indicates **place.***
- *Mark every reference to **Jesus,** including the words **You** and **Yourself.***
- *Underline every reference to **crucifixion** and **cross.***

Mark 15:22–32

22 Then they brought Him to the place Golgotha, which is translated, Place of a Skull.

23 They tried to give Him wine mixed with myrrh; but He did not take it.

24 And they crucified Him, and divided up His garments among themselves, casting lots for them to decide what each man should take.

25 It was the third hour when they crucified Him.

26 The inscription of the charge against Him read, "The King of the Jews."

27 They crucified two robbers with Him, one on His right and one on His left.

28 [And the Scripture was fulfilled which says, "And He was numbered with transgressors."]

29 Those passing by were hurling abuse at Him, wagging their heads, and saying, "Ha! You who are going to destroy the temple and rebuild it in three days,

INSIGHT

Jesus' crucifixion began at the third hour, about 9 a.m.

Just like scourging, *crucifixion* was a prolonged, sensational public torture designed to frighten people from committing crimes similar to the one for which the perpetrator was being punished. The Romans executed criminals on two types of cross: one was a simple vertical wood stake; the other the T-shape with the crossbeam (patibulum) that we are used to seeing.

Most scholars have concluded that Jesus was crucified on the T because the three-language inscription was "above His head" (Matthew 27:37), and this would have been impossible to read vertically.

Criminals that survived scourging were forced to carry the crossbeam to the place of execution, a place easily seen so passersby would be warned. Once there, the soldiers would find the hole-like depression you can feel in the middle of your wrist. A heavy iron nail would be driven through it deep into the crossbeam. The pain was excruciating, curling the hand because of damage to the nerve that runs through that hole. The victim was then lifted from the ground, hanging by the nails, as the crossbeam was dropped into the wedge of the upright. Dangling by his wrists, bones out of joint, unable to breathe, his feet were then nailed to the upright, knees flexed so he could push his bloody flesh and bones up against the rough bark of the cross. Otherwise he could not breathe. The suffocating carbon dioxide accumulating in his lungs had to be exhaled. Words would be few.

Crucifixion dislocated the bones, putting the victim's joints into tormenting muscle cramps, while the heart experienced its own compression. It seems from John 19:34 Jesus' heart literally ruptured—thus the "blood and water."

Thirst intensified as the body lost its fluid and blood. Victims that did not die from shock succumbed to suffocation as their legs were broken, and they could no longer breathe.

Cicero described it as "the cruelest and most hideous punishment possible."*

30 save Yourself, and come down from the cross!"

31 In the same way the chief priests also, along with the scribes, were mocking Him among themselves and saying, "He saved others; He cannot save Himself.

32 "Let this Christ, the King of Israel, now come down from the cross, so that we may see and believe!" Those who were crucified with Him were also insulting Him.

---

* *In Verrem* 5.64.165.

DISCUSS

• What happened to Jesus in verses 22–26, and what hour of the day did this take place?

• In verses 27–28, what happened? Why was it significant?

• In verses 29–30, what happened to Jesus? Who were the people involved?

• Discuss verses 31–32. Who was insulting Jesus and on what basis?

• What do you learn in verses 27 and 32 about those being crucified along with Jesus?

OBSERVE

As you read in the Insight box, the process of crucifixion resulted in increasing thirst and excruciating pain. Consider how Jesus was suffering physically as you read about the final moments of His crucifixion.

Leader: Read Mark 15:33–39 and John 19:30 aloud. Have the group…
  • *circle all references to* **time.**
  • *mark all references to* **Jesus.**

DISCUSS

• According to Mark, what did Jesus cry out at the ninth hour?

• Does Jesus' cry surprise you? Any thought as to why Jesus would say this?

• According to the gospel of John, what were Jesus' final words from the cross?

MARK 15:33–39

33 When the sixth hour came, darkness fell over the whole land until the ninth hour.

34 At the ninth hour Jesus cried out with a loud voice, "Eloi, Eloi, lama sabachthani?" which is translated, "My God, My God, why have You forsaken Me?"

35 When some of the bystanders heard it, they began saying, "Behold, He is calling for Elijah."

36 Someone ran and filled a sponge with sour wine, put it on a reed, and gave Him a drink, saying, "Let us see whether Elijah will

come to take Him down."

37 And Jesus uttered a loud cry, and breathed His last.

38 And the veil of the temple was torn in two from top to bottom.

39 When the centurion, who was standing right in front of Him, saw the way He breathed His last, he said, "Truly this man was the Son of God!"

John 19:30

Therefore when Jesus had received the sour wine, He said, "It is finished!" And He bowed His head and gave up His spirit.

• Look at John 19:30 again. What does this tell you about Jesus' death?

INSIGHT

"It is finished!" (John 19:30) is a translation of the single Greek verb *tetélestai,* a third-person perfect passive of the root *teléo* meaning "to bring to end, finish, complete, fulfill."

The action of a perfect tense originates in the past and is usually completed in the present. Thus Jesus' use of the perfect tense tells us that He has *completed* the work of reconciling men to God *on the cross.* Mankind's sins have been paid for in full through His sacrifice. (See also Ephesians 2:16; Colossians 1:20; 2:14; Hebrews 10:8–14; 1 Peter 2:24.)

OBSERVE

We are going to finish this week's study by looking at a portion of Psalm 22, believed to be a prophetic description of the agony of death by crucifixion and of Jesus' death in particular.

Keep in mind, crucifixion was not commonly used until the times of the Romans, centuries after David's reign.

Leader: *Read Psalm 22:1–3 aloud and have the group...*

- *mark every use of the words* ***my, me,*** *and* ***I*** *with a cross, like this:* ✝
- *mark every reference to* **God,** *including the word* **You,** *with a triangle:* △

DISCUSS

- In verses 1–2, what is the situation between God and the one crying to God?

- According to verse 3, how does the one crying out feel about God?

PSALM 22:1–3

1 My God, my God, why have You forsaken me? Far from my deliverance are the words of my groaning.

2 O my God, I cry by day, but You do not answer; and by night, but I have no rest.

3 Yet You are holy, O You who are enthroned upon the praises of Israel.

PSALM 22:6–18

6 But I am a worm and not a man, a reproach of men and despised by the people.

7 All who see me sneer at me; they separate with the lip, they wag the head, saying,

8 "Commit yourself to the LORD; let Him deliver him; let Him rescue him, because He delights in him."

9 Yet You are He who brought me forth from the womb; You made me trust when upon my mother's breasts.

10 Upon You I was cast from birth; You have been my God from my mother's womb.

OBSERVE

Leader: *Read Psalm 22:6–18. Have the group…*

- *continue to mark with a cross the references to* **the psalmist**—*the words* **I** *and* **me,** *and the lowercase occurrences of* **him** *in verse 8.*
- *mark with a triangle the references to* **the Lord** *(God the Father), including all pronouns, such as the capitalized* **Him** *in verse 8.*
- *underline every reference to* **men** *and* **the people,** *including pronouns and any synonyms such as* **bulls** *and* **dogs.**

DISCUSS

- List the similarities you see between Psalm 22 and the account of the crucifixion of Jesus.

• Look at verses 14–17. How does this description correspond to what happens to the body during crucifixion?

• Look at verses 9–11. How does the psalmist handle this trial, and what does this tell you about his relationship to God?

11 Be not far from me, for trouble is near; for there is none to help.

12 Many bulls have surrounded me; strong bulls of Bashan have encircled me.

13 They open wide their mouth at me, as a ravening and a roaring lion.

14 I am poured out like water, and all my bones are out of joint; my heart is like wax; it is melted within me.

15 My strength is dried up like a potsherd, and my tongue cleaves to my jaws; and You lay me in the dust of death.

16 For dogs have surrounded me; a band of

evildoers has encompassed me; they pierced my hands and my feet.

17 I can count all my bones. They look, they stare at me;

18 They divide my garments among them, and for my clothing they cast lots.

• By way of application, though we may never be killed for our faith, do you see anything here that can help you in times of trial or crisis?

WRAP IT UP

It was a unique day in the life of Simeon. This righteous and devout man had been looking for the consolation of Israel—Messiah. Now, prompted by the Spirit of God, he went to the temple on the very same day Joseph and Mary took their newborn son, Jesus, to present Him to the Lord.

When Simeon saw them, he knew it was the moment the Spirit had promised. Taking Jesus into his aged arms, he blessed God and said, "Now Lord, You are releasing Your bond-servant to depart in peace, according to Your word; for my eyes have seen Your salvation, which You have prepared in the presence of all peoples. A Light of revelation to the Gentiles, and the glory of Your people Israel" (Luke 2:29–32).

About thirty-three years later, the mission was accomplished. After three years of teaching and proclaiming His God-given mission of seeking and saving the lost, Jesus cried out on the cross, "It is finished!"

The death of Jesus on the cross secured salvation for the many. What appeared to be a tragic mistake in the slaying of the only perfectly righteous man turned out to be the victory over death. The will of God was accomplished, and we now are "sanctified through the offering of the body of Jesus Christ once for all.... For by one offering He has perfected for all time those who are sanctified" (Hebrews 10:10, 14). The only human being ever born without sin took our sin upon Himself. God made Jesus "who knew no sin to be sin on our behalf, so that we might become the righteousness of God in Him" (2 Corinthians 5:21).

He bore in His body each and every sin we ever have committed and will commit. Why? So that we who believe might be forgiven and declared righteous! So that we may be saved from sin's penalty and power—and someday live in God's presence with His Son.

Sin's debt has been paid in full. There is no other sacrifice to be made! The sacrifice of Jesus broke sin's power; you don't have to live in bondage any longer.

Have you truly believed this? If so, the way you live will show that Jesus Christ is in you, the hope of glory!

As Mark opens his gospel, he details the first recorded words of God in respect to Jesus: "You are My beloved Son, in You I am well pleased" (1:11).

As Mark brings his gospel to a close, he notes the words of the centurion who stood in front of the cross and watched Jesus take His last breath: "Truly this man was the Son of God!" (15:39)

What happened to God's beloved Son? Paul explains it this way: "Christ redeemed us from the curse of the Law, having become a curse for us—for it is written, 'Cursed is everyone who hangs on a tree'" (Galatians 3:13).

The curse we deserve was taken by the sinless Son of Man. And what does that mean? It means that in paying for our sin by His death, Jesus made powerless the devil, the one who had the power of death (Hebrews 2:14–15). Death could not hold Jesus in its grip, nor can it hold you if you believe that the Son of Man, Jesus Christ, is the Son of God (John 20:30–31).

That is why the resurrection of Jesus Christ is an essential element of the gospel. You'll find an account of it in each of the four Gospels. Let's see what Mark tells us.

MARK 15:40–47

40 There were also some women looking on from a distance, among whom were Mary Magdalene, and Mary the mother of James the Less and Joses, and Salome.

41 When He was in Galilee, they used to follow Him and minister to Him; and there were many other women who came up with Him to Jerusalem.

42 When evening had already come, because it was the preparation day, that is, the day before the Sabbath,

43 Joseph of Arimathea came, a prominent member of the

OBSERVE

In the closing verses of Mark 15, God tells us about the actions of some key people in the aftermath of Jesus' death. Let's see who they are and what God wants us to know about them.

Leader: Read Mark 15:40–47 aloud. Have the group listen carefully for what happens with each of the people in these scenes.

Leader: Read the text again and have the group do the following:

- *Circle references to **time**.*
- *Mark each occurrence of the word **women** (not individuals) with a **W**.*
- *Mark all references to **Jesus**.*
- *Mark references to **Joseph** with a big **J**.*
- *Put a box around the references to **Pilate**.*
- *Mark references to **the centurion** with a big **C**.*

DISCUSS

• What did you learn about each of the people you marked? How do their responses to Jesus' death differ from one another?

• What do these people have in common in respect to the crucifixion of Jesus?

Council, who himself was waiting for the kingdom of God; and he gathered up courage and went in before Pilate, and asked for the body of Jesus.

44 Pilate wondered if He was dead by this time, and summoning the centurion, he questioned him as to whether He was already dead.

45 And ascertaining this from the centurion, he granted the body to Joseph.

46 Joseph bought a linen cloth, took Him down, wrapped Him in the linen cloth and laid Him in a tomb which had been hewn out in the rock; and he rolled a stone against the entrance of the tomb.

⁴⁷ Mary Magdalene and Mary the mother of Joses were looking on to see where He was laid.

MARK 16:1–8

¹ When the Sabbath was over, Mary Magdalene, and Mary the mother of James, and Salome, bought spices, so that they might come and anoint Him.

² Very early on the first day of the week, they came to the tomb when the sun had risen.

³ They were saying to one another, "Who will roll away the stone

• Some people believe Jesus just passed out or swooned. How likely does that seem, in light of what you've just read and marked? Explain your answer.

OBSERVE

Leader: Read Mark 16:1–8 aloud. Have the group do the following:

• *Mark references to **the women** with a* **W.**

• *Put a halo over every reference to **the young man in a white robe,** including pronouns:* ⌒

• *Mark references to **Jesus.***

• *Circle references to **time.***

• *Double underline anything that indicates **where** something occurred.*

DISCUSS

• What happened with the women? What time of day did this take place?

• What were they told had happened to Jesus the Nazarene? Should they have been amazed by this? Why or why not?

• What in this study has amazed you the most?

• If you stopped right here in the gospel of Mark, how might what you've learned affect the way you celebrate Easter, and why?

for us from the entrance of the tomb?"

4 Looking up, they saw that the stone had been rolled away, although it was extremely large.

5 Entering the tomb, they saw a young man sitting at the right, wearing a white robe; and they were amazed.

6 And he said to them, "Do not be amazed; you are looking for Jesus the Nazarene, who has been crucified. He has risen; He is not here; behold, here is the place where they laid Him.

7 "But go, tell His disciples and Peter, 'He is going ahead of you to Galilee; there you will see Him, just as He told you.'"

8 They went out and fled from the tomb, for trembling and astonishment had gripped them; and they said nothing to anyone, for they were afraid.

INSIGHT

Thus ends the gospel of Mark—at least, this is the way the earliest manuscripts end. Mark concludes his gospel as abruptly as he began it. He gives us the gospel, the good news of Jesus Christ, Son of God (1:1–16:8), and stops. Mission accomplished!

However, because of its abrupt ending, some scholars believe the original ending of Mark was lost, others that Mark intended to finish this way. Still others believe Mark never finished his gospel. No one knows for certain.

Later manuscripts contain verses 9–20, although internal evidence (the style of writing, the vocabulary, grammar) suggests that these passages had a different writer.

OBSERVE

Let's familiarize ourselves with the remaining text of Mark as it appears in our Bibles, with the footnote that verses 9–20 were added to later manuscripts.

Leader: Read Mark 16:9–20 aloud. Have the group do the following:
- *Mark all references to **Jesus**.*
- *Circle any words that indicate **time** or a progression of events.*
- *Underline with an arrow every reference to **those who had been with Him**, beginning at verse 10.*
- *Put a check mark over each of **those who believe**: ✓*
- *Put an X over **those who do not believe**.*

DISCUSS

- What do you learn from these verses about Jesus and those He encountered after His resurrection? Discuss each event, following the sequence listed in the passage.

MARK 16:9–20

9 Now after He had risen early on the first day of the week, He first appeared to Mary Magdalene, from whom He had cast out seven demons.

10 She went and reported to those who had been with Him, while they were mourning and weeping.

11 When they heard that He was alive and had been seen by her, they refused to believe it.

12 After that, He appeared in a different form to two of them while they were walking along on their way to the country.

13 They went away and reported it to the

others, but they did not believe them either.

14 Afterward He appeared to the eleven themselves as they were reclining at the table; and He reproached them for their unbelief and hardness of heart, because they had not believed those who had seen Him after He had risen.

15 And He said to them, "Go into all the world and preach the gospel to all creation.

16 "He who has believed and has been baptized shall be saved; but he who has disbelieved shall be condemned.

17 "These signs will accompany those who

• What were Jesus' instructions to the eleven?

• In verse 16, what do you learn about those who believe and those who do not?

• According to these added verses, what various signs accompany those who believe?

INSIGHT

It is important that verses 17 and 18 be taught with great care, allowing scripture to interpret scripture. Remember scripture is God's Word; therefore, scripture will never contradict scripture, nor should some obscure interpretation take precedent over what is generally taught in the whole counsel of God. For instance, some have misused this text and have formed congregations (sects) that handle venomous snakes or drink poison as proof of their faith.

Not only are such actions not supported in any other place in the Word of God, Jesus said we are not to put God to the test (Matthew 4:7). The reality of our faith is not seen in deliberately placing our lives in danger; rather, according to Jesus, it is seen in the way we love others and in the fruit that comes from abiding in Jesus, the true vine (John 13:34–35; 15:8).

We suggest you read the final chapters of the other gospels when you have time. This way you can compare the encounters mentioned in verses 9–15 with the other gospel accounts.

What you want to remember is that all the Gospels have the account of the resurrection of Jesus Christ.

• What do verses 15 and 20 have in common, and how does verse 20 support the command of Jesus?

have believed: in My name they will cast out demons, they will speak with new tongues;

18 they will pick up serpents, and if they drink any deadly poison, it will not hurt them; they will lay hands on the sick, and they will recover."

19 So then, when the Lord Jesus had spoken to them, He was received up into heaven and sat down at the right hand of God.

20 And they went out and preached everywhere, while the Lord worked with them, and confirmed the word by the signs that followed.

MATTHEW 28:5–7, 16–20

⁵ The angel said to the women, "Do not be afraid; for I know that you are looking for Jesus who has been crucified.

⁶ "He is not here, for He has risen, just as He said. Come, see the place where He was lying.

⁷ "Go quickly and tell His disciples that He has risen from the dead; and behold, He is going ahead of you into Galilee, there you will see Him; behold, I have told you."…

¹⁶ But the eleven disciples proceeded to Galilee, to the mountain which Jesus had designated.

OBSERVE

Let's compare what you observed in Mark 16:15, 20 with the other synoptic gospels, Matthew and Luke.

Leader: Read Matthew 28:5–7, 16–20 and Luke 24:4–9, 44–49. Have the group do the following:

- *Mark all references to **Jesus,** including pronouns.*
- *Put an upward arrow over every reference to **Jesus' resurrection:** ↑*
- *Underline with an arrow all references to **the disciples,** including pronouns.*
- *Double underline anything that indicates **where.***

DISCUSS

- What do you learn from marking the references to Jesus in Matthew and Luke? Note the similarities.

17 When they saw Him, they worshiped Him; but some were doubtful.

18 And Jesus came up and spoke to them, saying, "All authority has been given to Me in heaven and on earth.

19 "Go therefore and make disciples of all the nations, baptizing them in the name of the Father and the Son and the Holy Spirit,

20 teaching them to observe all that I commanded you; and lo, I am with you always, even to the end of the age."

LUKE 24:4–9, 44–49

4 While they were perplexed about this, behold, two men suddenly stood near them in dazzling clothing;

5 and as the women were terrified and bowed their faces to the ground, the men said to them, "Why do you seek the living One among the dead?

6 "He is not here, but He has risen. Remember how He spoke to you while He was still in Galilee,

7 saying that the Son of Man must be delivered into the hands of sinful men, and be crucified, and the third day rise again."

8 And they remembered His words,

9 and returned from the tomb and reported all these things to the eleven and to all the rest....

• What do you learn from marking the references to the disciples? Move through the text verse by verse.

• Broadly speaking, what do you see that correlates with what you've observed in the gospel of Mark?

44 Now He said to them, "These are My words which I spoke to you while I was still with you, that all things which are written about Me in the Law of Moses and the Prophets and the Psalms must be fulfilled."

45 Then He opened their minds to understand the Scriptures,

46 and He said to them, "Thus it is written, that the Christ would suffer and rise again from the dead the third day,

47 and that repentance for forgiveness of sins would be proclaimed in His name to all the nations, beginning from Jerusalem.

48 "You are witnesses of these things.

49 "And behold, I am sending forth the promise of My Father upon you; but you are to stay in the city until you are clothed with power from on high."

---

1 CORINTHIANS 15:1–8

1 Now I make known to you, brethren, the gospel which I preached to you, which also you received, in which also you stand,

2 by which also you are saved, if you hold fast the word which I preached to you, unless you believed in vain.

3 For I delivered to you as of first importance what I also

OBSERVE

The apostle Paul wrote the majority of the New Testament epistles, or letters, to believers in the early church. Let's close our study by looking at what Paul wrote to those in Corinth in respect to the gospel of Jesus Christ.

Leader: Read 1 Corinthians 15:1–8 aloud. Have the group…

- *put a box around every reference to **the gospel,** including **which** and **what.***
- *mark all the references to **Jesus.***
- *draw an upward arrow over every reference to **the resurrection,** including Jesus' appearances after He was raised.*

DISCUSS

- What do you learn about the gospel from this passage? Beginning at verse 1, read through the text carefully so you don't miss a single truth.

- What do you learn from marking *Jesus*?

- According to this passage, what is the evidence of Jesus' death?

- What proves that Jesus was raised from death?

- Was Paul an eyewitness to what he wrote? How do you know?

- Do you believe the gospel? Why?

- How does this good news impact the way you are living? How are you sharing the message?

- Finally, how would what you learned this week impact your response if a doctor diagnosed you with an illness that might take your life?

received, that Christ died for our sins according to the Scriptures,

4 and that He was buried, and that He was raised on the third day according to the Scriptures,

5 and that He appeared to Cephas, then to the twelve.

6 After that He appeared to more than five hundred brethren at one time, most of whom remain until now, but some have fallen asleep;

7 then He appeared to James, then to all the apostles;

8 and last of all, as to one untimely born, He appeared to me also.

WRAP IT UP

Some would try to persuade us that there is no resurrection of the dead, even as some tried to convince the apostle Paul. His response? "If Christ has not been raised, your faith is worthless; you are still in your sins" (1 Corinthians 15:17).

Beloved, do you understand that because Jesus Christ rose from the dead, never to die again, if you believe you will do the same? Just think: you are going to spend eternity with the One who so loved you that He laid down His life for you!

When you become His disciple, His follower, you pass from death to life—life with a purpose, with abundance, with a mission (Matthew 28:18–20; John 10:10; Ephesians 2:10).

Jesus' final message to us in Mark is to "go into all the world and preach the gospel to all creation" (16:15). This is now *your* mission. Take what you have learned in the gospel of Mark and share it with others.

"How beautiful are the feet of those who bring good news of good things!" (Romans 10:15). The gospel of Jesus Christ is the good news of freedom to all who believe!

ABOUT KAY ARTHUR AND PRECEPT MINISTRIES INTERNATIONAL

KAY ARTHUR is known around the world as an international Bible teacher, author, conference speaker, and host of the national radio and television programs *Precepts for Life,* which reach a worldwide viewing audience of over ninety-four million. Recipient of the NRB Hall of Fame Award in 2011, Kay is a four-time Gold Medallion Award–winning author of more than one hundred books and Bible studies. She received an honorary doctorate from Tennessee Temple University.

Kay and her husband, Jack, founded Precept Ministries International in 1970 in Chattanooga, Tennessee, with a vision to establish people in God's Word. Today, the ministry has a worldwide outreach. In addition to inductive-study training workshops and thousands of small-group studies across America, PMI ministers in 180 countries with inductive Bible studies translated into more than seventy languages, discipling people by teaching them how to discover Truth for themselves.

ABOUT DAVID ARTHUR

DAVID ARTHUR serves as chief executive officer of Precept Ministries International. Having been mentored by his parents, Jack and Kay Arthur, in the value of inductive Bible study, he shares their passion for establishing people in God's Word.

Prior to his role at Precept, David worked in the business world with IBM and small businesses. Starting in 1999 David served for several years as a pastor in both the Presbyterian Church of America and the Associate Reformed Presbyterian Church. Just before coming to Precept, he was vice president with Generous Giving, working with givers and pastors. David is a passionate and gifted teacher of God's Word. He holds a bachelor's degree in organizational management from Covenant College and a master of arts in theological studies from Reformed Theological Seminary.

Contact Precept Ministries International for more information about inductive Bible studies in your area.

Precept Ministries International
PO Box 182218
Chattanooga, TN 37422-7218
800-763-8280
www.precept.org